T0132108

C for Curiosity

Lin Lim, Ph.D.

Archway Publishing books may be ordered through booksellers or by contacting:

Archway Publishing
1663 Liberty Drive
Bloomington, IN 47403
www.archwaypublishing.com
844-669-3957

ISBN: 978-1-6657-2744-0 (sc)
ISBN: 978-1-6657-2743-3 (e)

Print information available on the last page.

Archway Publishing rev. date: 08/15/2022

For my family,

who broadened my vision
to the outer boundaries
of human variability.

Marveling at the
Big

& small…

Wondering, what is Above

and Below

Below

Music EVERYWHERE,

Waiting to be heard

Paper transformed
to a square knight

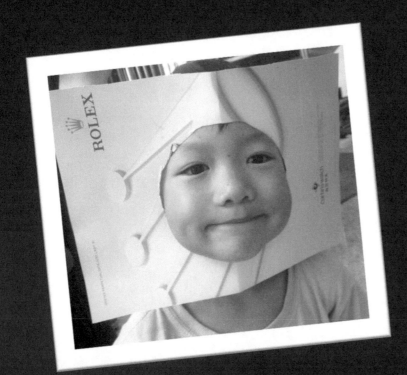

A plastic bag
turned backpack

L ⊙⊙ k!

Edible Art
as I wait

Reading opportunities abound,

from a Boba Tea Shop ...

to the
BOTANICAL
gardens...

Even when waiting

at the <u>airport</u>

Experiential learning,

highly recommended!

Time to make ...

a foil
sculpture garden

Still
Processing...

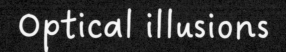

Optical illusions

Very funny

Out through the
TARDIS in a blink,

Right next to
221B Baker Street

Wandering about,

Wondering in
WONDER-LAND

Off the beaten path ...

often includes stopping on our way,
to another place

Pause to experience,

I FEEL this ship rocking!

Which leads me
to ponder,

"to bee, or not bee?"

Important to

RESET as necessary

Hmm...

What is in this "normal" store?

Will we fit?

Yes!

Yet greater joy,

when I am free
to create MY space

What are they trying to say?

Erm, Not sure

Looking through my lens

Things are crystal clear

Yet no words,

describe how I feel,
most times

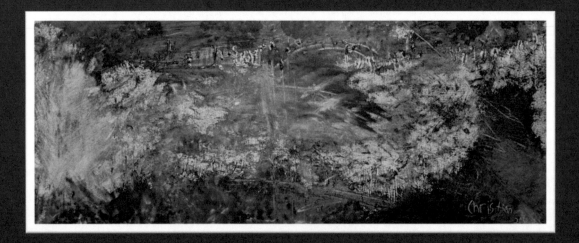

This is what
Handwriting
feels like,

do

see

you

my

Alphabets?

Trying to explain

Time Travel

Requires recharging...

battery ran out

Till next time ...

Stay Curious,

ZENLIVING.COM
Lifespan Health

Printed in the United States
by Baker & Taylor Publisher Services